Dr. Lothar Gassmann

Europe – a Dictatorship?

Is there still freedom of speech in Europe?

Author and Copyright:

Dr. Lothar Gassmann
Pforzheim
Germany
Email-Address: logass1@t-online.de
Homepage: www.L-Gassmann.de

English translator: Cynthia Muertter

Table of Contents

Introduction

The subject of my theses is: "Europe – a dictatorship? Is there still freedom of speech in Europe?-The non-discrimination laws and their consequences." I will be quoting very many sources. For, when addressing such a controversial subject it is good to let other sources do the speaking about the laws and decisions that are being made, not only in Europe but worldwide. I purposely begin with a non-European country to bring to awareness current global events and the strategies behind them.

The moral destruction of South Africa

Let us take a first look at South Africa. To begin, let it be said that this country has always had immense difficulties. The unrighteousness of the Apartheid and the separation of the blacks and the coloreds from the whites are examples, which were surely not Christian-like. Yet, that which has taken place in recent years in South Africa is at least as ungodly. Within a very short period of time, all Christian values and ethics which once existed have been overthrown, invalidated. Any mention of God was been removed from the constitution. Just as in Europe, one is only obliged to uphold core humanistic values. (In this manner, being there is no room for mentioning God; Europe forfeited her rich religious, cultural and humanistic inheritance.)

In the constitution of South Africa, humanism – the wisdom of men and the state, replaces "humble obedience to the almighty God", as it was written. Christianity is no longer favored and all religions are valued equally. Children are even being taught heathen practices in the schools. In 1996 a law prohibiting pornography, was changed to protect it under constitutional law! At the same time, abortion became legal, as it did in Germany and Switzerland.

In Exodus 20:13 God says: "Thou shalt not murder!"In South Africa abortion is allowed up until the 20th week of pregnancy. Millions of innocent, unborn children have been murdered since abortion was legalized in 1996.

The peak of the perversion of the South African legislation is that those who prevent an abortion, not the one who performs it, can be liable for of up to 10 years imprisonment. (UCA-News, United Christian Action, Cape Town, 20.04.2006).

Furthermore, in 2000, the non-discrimination law for the furthering of equality was passed. This law makes it illegal for anyone to injure or discriminate against another person based on their religion. The president of the ACDP, Pastor Kenneth Meshoe, criticizes this law, saying: "This law interferes with other rights that have also been put in writing; such as the freedom of faith, the freedom of religion, the freedom of speech and the freedom of conscience to name a few." The conflict between the non-discrimination law and the free expression of religion and the freedom to preach becomes very apparent. I will discuss this in more detail later. Additionally, South Africa is legalizing marriage for same-sex couples to include giving them the right to adopt children and undergo sex change operations. The age of consent for Sodomy has been lowered from 19 to 16 years of age. Prostitution is also allowed. One law regarding minors, allows 12-year old girls to abort a child without prior parental consent. This country is also preparing one of the most liberal laws known on Euthanasia. Holland has laws allowing for Euthanasia as well. I believe that by these laws there is real danger that a patients own will to live may be ignored.

Canada's Anti-Hate Laws

Let us now take a look at Canada and the following report in the World Net Daily, from 18.02.2003 written by Hugh Owens of Regina, Saskatchewan. In light of a planned, homosexual parade, Mr. Owens, printed an ad in a Canadian newspaper. This ad was a simple, picture of two men holding hands that had been crossed out, with a list of the bible verses (Rom. 1, Lev. 18:22, Lev. 20:13, I Cor. 6:9-10) next to it.

Anyone, familiar with the bible, knows that these are verses where God condemns homosexuality and other sexual perversions. Practically speaking, Owens simply had a picture with four bible verses published in a newspaper without any other added comments. What happened next? He was sentenced in 2003, by the Queen's Bench in Saskatchewan and fined for 4500 Canadian dollars. The verdict was – and I quote: "The slashed figures alone were not enough to communicate the hatred … but the addition of Bible references are more dangerous."

Another example shows the effect of a stand towards other religions, also taken from the World Net Daily, from 31.10.2002. The Canadian Pastor, Mark Harding, does not believe that Islam is a peaceful religion. The Koran was to be copied and distributed at his local high school. A room was also set up for Islamic students to meet and conduct their prayers during school hours. Pastor Harding protested. He simply protested, saying that he did not think this was right. He supported his protest by claiming that the bible also had something to say about this. What happened? Canada's Supreme Court passed a verdict on October 17, 2002 accusing him of purposefully spreading hatred. He was sentenced to two years probation and 340 hours of social labor at an Islamic community.

Next I will quote from some of the laws that were passed on April 30, 2003 by the Canadian Justice Department. Paragraphs 318 and 319 define Hate-propaganda and Genocide. In Paragraph 318 it says: "Every one who advocates or promotes genocide is guilty of an indictable offence and liable to imprisonment for a term not exceeding five years..." This includes public instigation to hatred as formulated in Paragraph 319: "Every one who, by communicating statements in any public place, incites hatred against any identifiable group where such incitement is likely to lead to a breach of the peace is guilty of (a) an indictable offence and is liable to imprisonment for a term not exceeding two years." And then it says: "Every one who, by communicating statements, other than in private conversation, willfully promotes hatred against any identifiable group is guilty of (a) an indictable offence and is liable to imprisonment for a term not exceeding two years."

The USA and the Homosexual Agenda

Janet L. Folger published an important novel in the USA in 2005 titled: "The Criminalization of Christianity". "Read this, before it becomes illegal!" was the subtitle. In it she writes: "The ultimate goal of the homosexual movement is the criminalization of Christianity."[1]

On pages 82 and 82 she makes publicly known a homosexual agenda that had been officially approved at a "Gay Pride March" in Washington D.C. on April 25, 1993. In summary these are the goals:

---

[1] J. L. Folger, The Criminalization of Christianity, Oregon 2005, p. 14

1. All laws prohibiting sodomy should be abolished and all forms of sexual expression should be legalized.

2. Demanded more funding for health care for AIDS victims and to support sex change operations. (Some time ago in the US a female, Methodist minister had herself changed to a male.)

3. Same sex marriage should be legalized along with their right to adopt children.

4. Homosexual education should be introduced and offered at all levels to include elementary schools.

5. Birth Control and abortion services should be available to everyone regardless of age.

6. Tax money should be used to provide artificial insemination for lesbians and bisexuals.

7. Religious-based comments (or objections) should be made prohibited.

8. Organizations like the boy scouts must be forced to allow homosexual group leaders.

Naturally, we want to help individuals with homosexual tendencies with godly counseling, and support them to find their way to a natural, God intended heterosexuality. This is God's creation plan, and HIS command.

I see all of this as clear signs of the approaching last days where the man of perdition (sin) more and more seeks to set himself upon God's throne. Not only by the propagation of immorality, but at the same time attempting to "tame" and silence the so-called "fundamentalists".

The UN and UNESCO against Fundamentalism

The expression "to tame" the fundamentalists comes from Mr. Robert Muller. Robert Muller, a native of Alsace, was the vice-secretary of the United Nations for 30 years. He has been working on a "one world government" and a "one world church" for a long time. "My dream", he says, "is to get a tremendous alliance between all the major religions and the United Nations". Muller is a typical New Age thinker. He works toward this goal, together with Theosophists in the traditions of Blavatsky and Besant.[2] He goes on to say: "Peace can only be possible though the taming of fundamentalism". He literally means those Christians who hold fast to the Holy Scriptures as the divinely inspired Word of God as it is written (at least in its original texts).[3]

The United Religions Initiative (URI) said in the year 2000: "Members of the URI shall not be coerced to participate in any ritual or to proselytize."[4] What is meant by proselytizing here is the process of inviting someone to convert by telling them: "You must become a Christian, or you will be lost." This is another expression for evangelizing. So, in other words, this should be repressed. On one hand lawlessness should be allowed to increase while on the other hand, those who proclaim the word of God by saying, "this is NOT God's will!" should be silenced.

It is also significant to mention the UNESCO's Declaration on the Principles of Tolerance. Therein it states: "Tolerance ... upholds human rights, pluralism ... It involves the rejection of dogmatism and

---

[2] L. Gassmann, Wendezeit 2000. What hides behind the New Age?, Lage, 3 edit. 2008
[3] Quote from J.L.Folger, p. 94
[4] Ibid p. 95

absolutism", which is the same as fundamentalism here. Further: "It also means that ones views are not to be imposed on others."[5]

Here I raise an objection. There is a big difference between intolerance toward people and intolerance toward a subject matter. As Christians, we love and respect those who think differently than we do. Yet, if we are truly Christians and are serious about our faith, we can not be silent about the saving truth of the gospel of our Lord Jesus Christ. An undeniable conflict arises between a humanistic, tainted demand for an all-inclusive tolerance and the biblical directive of the Gospel to testify of the truth in Jesus Christ, who alone is the truth.

This UN declaration even speaks of "mental genocide". We all agree that physical genocide must be rejected. In this UN declaration they also reject genocide: "... killing members of a group", but it goes on to state: It is also condemnable if some one harms someone else mentally.[6] What is meant by a "mental harm"? Does this include quoting scriptures as was done in the first example I mentioned? Does it include wearing a button or sticker that proclaims Christ sovereignty? Should this be prohibited worldwide?

Freedom of Speech in England?

Now, let us look at Europe. Harry Hammond, a 67 year old Englishman, held up a sign in an English Park which said, "Stop immorality! Stop homosexuality! Stop lesbianism!" This was reported everywhere in the media. What happened? Homosexuals saw this, called one another on the phone and approached him in groups. At first they just made fun of him, but eventually they began to assault and beat this 67 year old brother to the ground. After that, they even called the police. Whom did the police end up arresting? They arrested this 67 year old brother! Then they charged him saying that his sign was illegal. His signed provoked people and that is not allowed anymore.[7]

The threat of imprisonment for Christians in Sweden

In the fall of 2002, Sweden passed a law by an overwhelming majority that plans to penalize critical comments about homosexuality or homosexuals with up to 4 years confinement. This will also apply when the person making the comment uses passages from the bible to support his stand. (Like Romans 1:26, I Corinthians 6:9-11 and others) It is legal to quote the bible, but it may no longer be interpreted and preached as something applicable to our modern day. It (the bible) should be reduced to the historical archives or a piece of historical literature. (Or should we say discriminated against?) We see that these are the plans of the devil and his adversary to draw us away from God and His Word and to isolate and persecute those who hold fast to God's Word.

Regarding the law in Sweden mentioned above, there was a test case. The Pastor of a non-denominational church named Ake Green, called homosexuality and other abnormal tendencies in one of his preaching's "a cancerous growth on the body of society". He went on to say that anyone who turns to Jesus and His strength, could be healed from these things. Someone pressed charges against

---

[5] Declaration of Principles of Tolerance, proclaimed and signed by the member states of the UNESCO, 16.11.1995 as quoted by J.L. Folger, p. 96
[6] See J.L. Folger p.97
[7] Ibid

Ake Green. After multiple appeals, this brother finally won his case in the highest Swedish Court. The Court decided that his comments are covered under the laws that grant the freedom of religion and the freedom of opinion. As a result the liberal parties in Sweden are striving to make this non-discrimination law even stricter. As it stands, however this case remains a test case that can be referred to as needed in future incidents.

The European Treaties and its Legislation

We will discuss the European Treaties and its Legislation. It is common knowledge that there is dispute over the Treaty of Lisbon. "Die Welt", a German newspaper has printed several articles on the subject from Roman Herzog, together with Luder Gerken. Roman Herzog is not just anybody. He was the Federal President of Germany from 1994 to 1999. From 1987 to 1994 he was the President of the German High Court. He even worked for the EU Charter by leading the commission that drafted the EU Charter. And what does he say about it now? "The European Union is a danger to Germany's parliamentary democracy." Furthermore he says, "People in Germany know more than some politicians might think. Most people are positive about the idea of a European integration as compared to the way things had been historically. Yet, at the same time an ominous feeling is creeping over them that something is not quite right. Somehow a mammoth-sized institution is arising, that is detached from the problems and traditions of the individual countries, yet simultaneously, taking more and more authority upon itself." In his articles he brings up the issue of the centralization of authority. This balling together of power is something that various countries have already experienced in the past. The former President goes on to stress, "the responsibility of a democracy is to keep things in check and balance and this is not happening. This can not continue this way!"[8]

We read the following in the preamble of the Treaty of the European Union: "DRAWING INSPIRATION from the cultural, religious and humanist inheritance of Europe, from which have developed the universal values of the inviolable and inalienable rights of the human person, freedom, democracy, equality and the rule of law". Where do this drawing and inspiration come from? Does it come from God's word? Does it come from Christianity? Is there any mention of God's important, central role as Lord? No, rather man is at the center. Man is the focal point. There is not one word about God. If that is the foundation of the new Europe, then we all know where this is heading.

The values of the Union are described in Article 2. What are these values? "The Union is founded on the values of respect for human dignity, freedom, democracy, equality, the rule of law and respect for human rights, including the rights of persons belonging to minorities. These values are common to the Member States in a society in which pluralism, non-discrimination, tolerance, justice, solidarity and equality between women and men prevail." At first glance this reads positively. Though anyone familiar with current world views, will clearly see the hand print of the Free Masons and their ideology of tolerance with no absolutes. The only absolute for them is humanism, man upon the throne. All religions are equal with no absolute way to God. It is noteworthy, that it is the Frenchman, Valery Giscard d'Estaing, a high level mason, who is primarily responsible for the content of the Treaty of the European Union, which was negotiated behind closed doors. I will yet prove this. In any event we now have an atheistic humanism being declared as obligatory without any mention of God or our occidental Christian heritage.

---

[8] R. Herzog/L. Gerken, "Die Europäische Union gefährdet die parlamentarische Demokratie in Deutschland", in: WELT AM SONNTAG Nr. 2 from 14.1.2007, p.8f.

A Co-worker of the "Bekenntnis movement in Westfalen", Gerhard Becker, wrote the following commentary: "The goal of humanism is a humanity without God. It is the moral foundation of socialism. Thus it is visible, that the European Convent is paving the way for a socialistic Europe. With Socialism not needing God, it is obvious that its spokesmen do not want any mention of HIM in their treaty. Without accountability to God it is impossible to govern the people of Europe in a manner that serves their good and functions to their benefit."[9]

Non-discrimination and its consequences

The issue of non-discrimination appears beneficial at first glance. I do not want to discriminate anybody by way of railing, or name calling or looking down at them with disgust and belittlement. But it is already considered discrimination when the Bible is quoted. God Himself is being presented as a discriminator. How far indeed things have come! God has only our very best in mind. He wants to save people and deliver them from their sins. God wants man to repent and turn from their sin. In Article 21 of the EU Charter it says; "Any discrimination based on any ground such as sex, race, color, ethnic or social origin, genetic features, language, religion or belief, political or any other opinion, membership of a national minority, property, birth, disability, age or sexual orientation shall be prohibited."

As one notices, the term "sexual orientation" is always at the end of the list. It is also no secret that homosexual groups are the driving forces behind the push for these kinds of laws to their advantage. The other listed items are just decoration to cover up the actual goal, namely lawful protection of sexual preference. All of the other mentioned rights for the handicapped, people of other religions etc are already been protected under most Basic Law. Only the sexual preference element is not protected and was earlier even punishable by law!

Is it the purpose of these new laws that one man may no longer say things like in John 14:6? There Jesus tells us that there is no other way to God, the Father than by Him: Jesus Christ. If we proclaim this message are we discriminating someone by negating their faith? Are we discriminating, when we tell someone that they must forsake their sins or they are lost? (To include the sins of pedophilia and any kind of sexual perversion like sodomy and homosexuality) This is a serious development! This would make missions and evangelizing very difficult, even illegal. This leaves us with a "soft" gospel where sin is no longer sin, and false teaching is no longer false teaching. Then we automatically have things like the "code of conduct for conversions" as a result to make it clear what should say, and what no longer may be said. I will discuss this "code for conduct" later.

---

[9] G. Becker, Die moralische Grundlage Im Entwurf einer Verfassung für Europa, in: BWL, Sept. 2004, p. 11.

The European Council condemns the biblical Creationism

The following passages will more clearly proof that the European Union is becoming more and more anti-christian. On October 4, 2007, a parliamentary session of the European Council released a resolution, titled: "The Dangers of Creationism in the Education." Creationism is the biblical teaching that God created the world in six days and on the seventh day HE rested, as His Word, the Holy Scriptures tells us (Gen 1 and 2). The repetition of the words: "...and there was evening and there was morning..." is a clear indicator that God created the world in six 24-hour days. Without doubt God, as Almighty Lord, could have made the world in seconds. God, however, established an order that gave us the seven day week. Everything has its purpose.

How was it formulated in this resolution? Take note how political bodies interfere with world viewpoints and faith-based decisions. Politicians determine what may be taught in schools concerning this subject. It is said: "If we are not careful, creationism could become a threat to human rights, which are the key concern of the Council of Europe." So here we have it. Just as in the days of the old Roman Empire, we are enemies of humanity if we still take the Bible seriously. It is understandable why many Christians speak of the end times. The end shall be as in the beginning.

Further is says: "Creationism can not lay claim to being a scientific discipline." I ask you, can evolution do that either? There is just as much of a belief system behind evolution as creationism; and that is atheism. There are fossil discoveries that could be interpreted as proof for creationism as well as for evolution. Again, there is a political body prescribing to us by what theory a fossil-find may be categorized.

Continuing on, this resolution says: "The theory of evolution has nothing to do with divine revelation, but is built on facts." Here we have it in black and white. Is it really possible that these politicians have never heard of the many inconsistencies that exist in the theory on evolution that scientists worldwide point out? Next it becomes graver: "Denying it could have serious consequences for the development of our societies … The war on the theory of evolution and on its proponents most often originates in forms of religious extremism which are closely allied to extreme right-wing political movements. The creationist movements possess real political power. The fact of the matter, and this has been exposed on several occasions, is that the advocates of strict creationism are out to replace democracy by theocracy."

Now you have it. As faithful, bible-believing Christians, we are being placed into the same ranks as the Nazis. I am anything but a Nazi. I have translated the Israeli national anthem into German and done other things for Israel. Yet we see how quickly they will corner us.

These are very serious developments. It is also clear why Christians need to be divided; the fundamentalists from the mediocre Christians. In section 14 of this resolution – here is a quote from non other than from the European Council: "All leading representatives of the main monotheistic religions have taken on a much more moderate viewpoint. The pope, Benedict XVI and his predecessor John Paul II praise the role that science plays in the evolution of man and acknowledge the theory on evolution as more than just a hypothesis." (A quote from Pope Benedict XVI)

What steps does the European Council require? What may be taught in schools in Europe? In § 19: "The Parliamentary Assembly calls on education authorities in member States to promote scientific knowledge and the teaching of evolution based on facts … and to oppose firmly any attempts at teaching creationism as a scientific discipline." Creationism is to be resisted. It should be limited to the area of religion. Kant has said: "One must make a clear separation between beliefs and knowledge:" This is not feasible. "….to promote the teaching on evolution as solidly founded scientific theory." This is what is to be strongly promoted in the new Europe, the re-emerging roman empire (as the fourth beast, as depicted by the prophet Daniel).[10]

Citizens desire the teaching on Creationism

In the summer of 2007 a German news show took a poll on the Internet, which was completed on July 24th 2007. The Question in this poll was: "Should the Christian teaching on Creation be included in biology classes, as demanded by the minister of education in Hessen, Karin Wolf and Bishop Walter Mixa?" The final poll results were: Of the 42,824 participants, no small number, 68.4% voted "YES" and 31% "NO". Two-thirds of those that participated want creationism taught alongside evolution. But in none of the newspapers I read, published these poll results in their paper. Admitted this poll can not be considered an official survey because it was possible for anyone to vote over the Internet.

However the organization Pro Genesis, also conducted an official poll in the summer of 2007. This organization is also planning a Creation Park in Europe. It ordered this Survey to be officially done in Switzerland. Therein the question was: "In your opinion, what should be taught in school biology classes, on the origins of life? a) Only Evolution, b) Only Creationism, c) Both equally?" The Answer was: Only Evolution: 19.5%, Only Creationism: 4.8%, but both equally: 75.6%. So people want their children to be able to form their opinion, by comparing both sides. I find this to be correct and the government should abide to the will of the people. We don't necessarily want only creationism taught, but the students should have the opportunity to learn about the Alternatives.

The EU-Treaty and the Incapacitation of its Citizens

Where do things stand at present in Europe? It is common knowledge that the Treaty of the EU was signed in October 2004 under a large statue of a pope. However, this treaty was voted down by two European countries. Oddly enough, and humbling as well, these countries were France and the Netherlands, where the greater majority of the Fathers of this treaty reside. In 2005 there was an informal survey taken by a larger newspaper in Germany. Approximately 95% of the Germans asked were against the EU Treaty. Why was this? Because the people realize that they are confronted with a mammoth-sized bugaboo, something eerie, whose developments are getting out of control, as Roman Herzog, a German Politician has also assessed. I again refer to the Title of the article in the WELT. "The European Union is a danger for the parliamentary democracy in Germany." Roman Herzog says that 84% of all jurisdictional decisions are already made in Brussels and Strasburg and no longer in Berlin. 84% is dictated to us at the European level![11]

An information service "TOPIC" in the issue number 11/2007, titled an article on page 5: "The EU reformed Treaty: Now harsher anti-discriminatory laws will be brought down on us." The prior Treaty

---

[10] L.Gassmann Europe-the re-emerging Roman Empire?, Lage, 3rd ed. 2008
[11] R. Herzog/L. Gerken, "Die Europäische Union gefährdet die parlamentarische Demokratie in Deutschland", in: WELT AM SONNTAG Nr. 2 form 14.1.2007, p. 8

of the EU is now the EU Reformed Treaty (Treaty of Lisbon; see the appendix in this book). In this Treaty they deviously added a 'link', as we say in the computer language, authorizing with the acceptance of the EU Reform Treaty the simultaneous acceptance of the EU Charter, which the people never "blessed".(or approved). Do we notice something here? All this things are taking place behind the backs of the average citizen. And of course, it contains no references to God. Here is a quote from the Prime Minister of Luxembourg, Jean Claude Juncker as taken from an Interview with the Spiegel on 16.06.2003. (This was at the time when the original Treaty was signed). Quote: "The proclamation was that this convent would be the biggest show of democracy. I have never seen a darker chamber of darkness then this convent." This was said by the Prime Minister of Luxembourg! He is by no means an unimportant figure in theses matters.

The Reverend Reinhard Moeller wrote an article titled, "The EU Citizen- Deceived, Betrayed, and Sold". He is talking about "Lisbon's black Friday – October 19, 2007." He goes on, "This new Treaty eliminated the individual countries' right to veto in 60 points. This is a relinquishing of national sovereignty. This seems to alarm no one in the German republic, but in Great Britain the people are in an uproar."[12]

Charles Moore from „The Daily Telegraph" comments on this and I purposely quote this. I, myself would not put it so sharply, yet I will say what a Brit says in a famous daily newspaper mostly about the politicians who are in charge: "The EU is not such a sharp oppression as was Soviet Communism, but it is similar in this respect - it tries wherever possible to avoid the democratic judgment of the people it rules. When that judgment does come, therefore, it will be merciless."[13]
I call no one to a hateful revolt. But I compel all of us to pray, to act and to not be silent as long as we, as citizens of this country and as Christians, yet, have the freedom to speak before it is too late concerning these laws.

An Anti-Christian Inquisition

The appointed Italian EU Commissioner, Rocco Buttiglione - a catholic and advisor to the Pope - was reprimanded by the an EU special committee and was not elected into the EU Commission because of his conservative stand on marriage and the traditional family, and his rejection of homosexuality, which he, being a catholic, considers sinful. Buttiglione sees himself as a victim of – as he puts it - an anti-christian Inquisition. He says this as a catholic, whose church itself conducted bloody inquisitions for hundreds of years! Buttiglione sees the threatening danger that Christians will be forbidden to work in various occupations as it was and is under communism and Islam. The effects of the laws of non-discrimination can also prove very threatening. What does "discrimination" actually mean? This word comes from the Latin word - discrimen, which means difference. One differentiates between good and bad, true and false which is right to do. However, presently the word "discrimination" is understood to put someone down and despise them. Of course as Christians we reject this kind of attitude and conduct. We do not want to degrade anyone down by slander, or evil speaking.

---

[12] R. Moeller, EU Bürger: belogen, verraten und verkauft, ZEITJOURNAL Nr. 4/2007, p. 28f.
[13] http://www.telegraph.co.uk/comment/3643450/Brussels-dictatorship-will-face-day-of-reckoning.html

When will it be unlawful to call sin "sin"?

An important question now arises: at what point can the allegation of discrimination be made? Will the standards of the secular population, the media, the people or the politicians thereby be justified? Will it be considered discrimination or slander when we as Christians call those lifestyles and attitudes evil or wrong as God and His word say they are? Is it unlawful to declare false teachings, sects and occult influences as wrong and unbiblical? Is it unlawful to tell people that they are lost if they do not turn from their sinful ways and turn to Jesus? Is it unlawful to confess Jesus Christ as the only Lord and redeemer? Those following the various religions and sects, and homosexuals whom we warn of God's pending judgment may feel discriminated when we direct them to concrete bible passages that tell us God's commandments (and restrictions) concerning these matters. In Leviticus 18, Romans 1, I Corinthians 6 and many other parts of the bible reveal that specific sexual practices are very clearly in God's eyes SIN, even abominable, to include homosexuality, incest, polygamy and sodomy. If it then becomes unlawful to call sin "sin", then for all practical purposes it is impossible to carry out the work of missions and evangelism. Because it is only possible for truth, righteousness and mercy to shine forth, with a backdrop of the wrong and sinful. We can not speak of the love of God and His redemption without telling about that from which God has redeemed us, and what this love cost HIM. What else should God forgive but our sins?? What should He deliver us from, except from the power of sin? The reformers always spoke of the contrasts: the law and the gospel, sin and grace. It is by the mercy of God that man experiences the forgiveness of sin. Only the repentant sinner, who has come to Jesus because his sins torment him, receives and perceives forgiveness.

Why we want to help homosexuals by counseling

I want to say a few things about homosexuality for a better understanding. It is not my purpose to discriminate against these people. For me, it is a problem that needs spiritual counseling. The act of homosexuality is sin, but so are greed, envy, haughtiness and many other things according to God's righteous standards. We do not want to point our finger at certain kinds of sins or sinners. Nor do we condemn those who sin, but we do condemn the sinful lifestyle that they love to live out; homosexuality being an example. We must tell those who practice such things, that this is not God's will. This must also be clear for the unbeliever who does not know the bible. If homosexuality had been God's will as the creator, mankind would have become instinct. This was not God's plan nor His will. "Be fruitful and multiply" is what His command was to his creation. (Genesis 1:28) Therefore it is absurd to equate the love between a man and a woman, with the love that same-sex couples may have, not to mention granting homosexual couples the right to adopt children. Again, we do not want to discriminate against homosexuals, but rather help them by godly counseling. This of course, can not successfully take place if the lifestyle is made equal to a normal marriage, thereby legalizing sin. The bible clearly calls homosexuality - sin. As Christians we want to see sinners saved. We can not just cover up sin. What kind of doctor would one be, if a seriously ill person was simply declared "healthy" and let to go his own way?

Christians, second class citizens?

Again I quote Buttiglione, the Italian commissioner and a counselor to the pope. I am purposely quoting a catholic, although I have very critical questions about catholic theology. As mentioned earlier, Buttiglione was disqualified for the position of EU commissioner on the basis of his conservative catholic, ethical beliefs, some aspects of which are biblical. He warns of a coming European „police force for moral conscience", he also sees "a second-class citizenship for Christians", if this brand marking of biblical views continues. He writes:

„This committee went even so far as to transgress into areas of a man's moral conscience by insisting that anyone, who demoralizes homosexuality, is not qualified for the office of an EU Commissioner. This means that all those who uphold the ethical standards of most Christian Churches, should be considered second-class citizens. By this standard of measure, the three founding fathers of the EU would not be "good enough"; Konrad Adenauer, Robert Schuman and Alcide de Gasperi. (As these three stood under the influence of the Christian Church; author's comments) ...agnostics not willing to accept that one's religiosity, and differing, moral standards do not disqualify them from a public office....if the European Parliament ...following the logic of my case- makes my disqualification a standard for a consequential, political policy - then they are on the best way of creating moral police force, and introducing a modern inquisition that gravely injures the rights to our freedom of religion and our freedom of conscience."[14]

The Inquisition – derived a Latin word meaning to question – was an instrument used by the Catholic Church to deal with "heretics", by means of torture and burnings at the stake. A heretic was anyone who deviated from the catholic teaching, even if it was only in a minor fashion. It is interesting that Buttiglione, himself a catholic, would accuse the EU of this tendency towards anyone who thinks different that they do. Buttiglione also criticizes the totalitarianism of so called liberals. Most liberals are not liberal at all. (Liberal means one who is open minded and not strict in the observances of orthodox, traditional, or established forms or ways) If they were truly liberal, they would also tolerate the conservatives. They are not liberal in this sense; thusly the so-called liberals are only interested in the relativism of morals and ethics. I, myself, have experienced brutal attacks from liberal church representatives. Buttiglione writes:

"The term "liberal" has taken on a second meaning. A liberal is actually someone who differentiates between ethics and politics and sacrifices themselves for the freedom of opinion, even if his own opinion differs. Some liberals, who have informed me of their solidarity, have this attitude. There is, however, another group of liberals, who basically represent a new atheistic religion. They only have one principle. There is only one truth and that is that there are no truths."[15]

The Dictatorship of Relativism

Professor Joseph Ratzinger, the current Pope Benedict XVI, talked about the dictatorship of relativism. (Even if the papal office is not biblical, the expression is).[16]. Relativism dictates that no absolute truths are allowed. This is another area where the EU is in danger of becoming a dictatorship. A further quote

---

[14] R. Buttiglione, Europas Gewissenspolizei, from Erneuerung und Abwehr, 2/2005 p.12
[15] R. Buttiglione, Der Totalitarismus der falschen Liberalen, in: Erneuerung und Abwehr Nr. 2 / 2005, S. 42.
[16] Lothar Gassmann, Kleines Katholizismus-Handbuch, Schacht-Audorf 2006, p. 119-138

from Buttiglione: "All, who believe in a firm set of values, present a danger to democracy, in their view."[17] This is the club that they will use to beat down all who believe in a firm set of foundational values, like bible-believing Christians, by labeling them Fundamentalists. This itself would bring about a persecution from the so-called democrats? (Could this not also be considered discrimination?) Buttiglione goes on to say: "In opposition, I would say that a society not committed to any set of values is a greater threat to democracy. This lack of values is the greatest threat to western democracy."[18]

How it becomes possible for anyone to be arrested at anytime

Next, I want to draw our attention to the European Arrest Warrant (EAW). This warrant severely endangers our freedom and democracy. Even in the last days there will be mission work, revivals and people turning to the Lord Jesus, but there will also be an increase in seductions and persecutions. The current draft of the European Arrest Warrant went into effect in 2005. This warrant can be applied to 32 obscurely defined crimes that can have multiple interpretations. (That is the dangerous part.) Amongst others listed are Terrorism, environmental crimes, xenophobia, and racism.[19] The danger lies in the fact, that these terms can be bent to applied to many given situations. For example, if someone rejects Islam as false, they could be charged for racism if they speak this openly.

Other guidelines set down by the EAR, make these crimes not just punishable in the country where they were committed, but they are punishable throughout Europe. For all practical purposes this means that if I say something that is not considered discriminatory in my own country, I could still be extradited to the country where this is punishable, even if it should be the only country where this is illegal. It could also happen that I can be sentenced for the same crime in multiple EU countries, one after the other. At the same time they can confiscate my assets, so that I can not afford a lawyer. All it would take is a mere allegation coming from that country. This could be a possible application of this European Arrest Warrant.

Will Europe become a brutal dictatorship?

The consequences of the European arrest warrant, is that any European citizen runs the risk of being liable for breaking a law of another country unawares, as it is not likely to know all of the laws of every land. Consequently, it is possible to have all of our civil liberties taken away, especially the freedom of speech. Thus the EU will become a brutal dictatorship as the Soviet Union and other federations once were. This knowledge coincides with that of other critical observers. Ulrich Skambraks, publisher of an information service ("TOPIC") writes the following:

"The foundation of any modern dictatorship is laid when it becomes possible to criminalize its citizens at a whim. (By means of stretching laws at random to declare one guilty, thereby silencing them by intimidation; comment by the writer). From this point of view it is important to think about what kind of apparatus was created by the EAW. This could be very effective in the fight against crime and terrorism. But the EAW makes it is possible for any European citizen to be arrested and incarcerated on

---

[17] Erneuerung und Abwehr, Nr. /2005, p. 42
[18] Ibid
[19] See also Erneuerung und Abwehr Nr. 2/2005, p. 54

any kind of dubious allegations, especially accusations of discrimination."[20]

Carlo Alberto Agnoli, an Italian lawyer and former judge, published a leaflet titled: "The EAW- the shortest path to tyranny." He writes:

"Anyone who has any kind of education in law, philosophy, or history, knows that the ground for a modern totalitarianism is laid by way of criminalizing as many of its subjects as possible. (Declaring someone to be a criminal or outlaw). When all become guilty then all can be condemned. If it is possible for anyone to be condemned than it is possible to crush any dissidents (someone having different views) at any time."[21]

Knowing that the data of every EU citizen is saved in a large computer in Brussels it is apparent how tight the controls are and with what ease anyone can be traced.

Why Most of the Churches Stand Powerless Against These Developments

How can the Christian churches take a stand against these developments? Although there are differences, one has to say that the majority of the larger Christian churches have themselves compromised and undermined, both politically and morally, those truths they were meant to uphold. This in part is a result of: a) their own critical stand on the bible, b) shameful worldliness, and c) a false ecumenism. All three of these points could be a lecture in themselves.

Ecumenism, since the II Vatican Council and the Assisi's prayer for peace in 1986, extends far beyond the inter-confessional, Christian church to include all of the religions of the world. The "Nostra Aetate" and "Lumen Gentium", declarations of the II Vatican Council allot even heathen religions some elements of truth, including the audacious supposition that Christians and Muslims pray to the same God. The Catholic Church made these claims under modern influences as early as the II Vatican Council (1962-1965). Representatives of the Lutheran churches, and even some evangelicals do not differ in their stand as well.

On the contrary it is very clear in I John 2:22-23, "Who is the liar but the one denies that Jesus is the Christ? This is the antichrist, the one who denies the Father and the Son. Whoever denies the Son does not have the Father; the one who confesses the Son has the Father also." Mohammad denied that Jesus is the Son of God and acknowledges him only as a prophet.

It is written in I Corinthians 10:20, "No, but I say that the things which the Gentiles sacrifice, they sacrifice to demons, and not to God." This truth applies to the heather religions. Without a doubt, there are people in these religions who have questions, and are seeking the truth and a purpose in life. But the revelation that alone brings salvation, is only found in God's word; the bible, and in God's Son; the Lord Jesus Christ. There are numerous publications available on this subject that give light to various questions on this subject from a biblical standpoint.

---

[20] Ibid, U. Skambraks p.16
[21] Ibid p, 19

The Roman Catholic church, along with other denominational and non-denominational churches, by expanding the Ecumenical movement to other religions, have relativized the truth, thus forfeiting any ability to take a critical stand on these matters concerning the laws of non-discrimination.

God's first commandment in Exodus 20:2 was: "You shall have no other gods besides me"! This was the bible quote of the year in 1986, the first time that this 'prayer for peace' in Assisi took place. It was a spiritual gathering of representatives from the various Christian confessions, and heathen religions to include the Dalai Lama, medicine men, Shamans, and other worshipers of ancestral spirits to 'pray' for peace. In reality, it was a pact with the devil to ask for a demonic 'peace'. (Please compare I Corinthians 10:20)! How is it possible to render Christian obedience to the great commission with that kind of fraternization? (Matthew 28)? Because of these kinds of examples, Christians, who hold to the infallibility of the whole word of God, are more and more being tagged as fundamentalists. Today, well known men of the faith like Luther, Calvin, Zwingli, Menno Simons, Spurgeon and others would be considered Fundamentalists as well.

The Destruction of the Protestant Faith

Many protestant churches have deviated from their Christian ethics. Some churches even allow the 'sanctification' of homosexual couples. How can something be blessed that God calls sin, even an abomination, something HE can never bless? It is noteworthy how many people are blinded today despite an education in theology. Or is this even a result of their so called theological education? Though there may be some positive aspects of a study in theology, many fundamental elements of the faith are being destroyed by that which is taught at the universities. Current modern trends toward biblical criticism, feminist theology, and logical interpretations greatly influence the destruction of a sound biblical foundation, by putting into question the sovereignty of God's Word. The importance of the pure and unchanged Word of God is replaced with inner psychic experiences and other modern influences.

What is fundamentalism?

Let us address the question: what does the term fundamentalism really mean? It is not only in the Christian sector that we are confronted with this expression. Principally, a fundamentalist is someone who, without compromise, supports and stands for certain fundamentals or basic principles without wavering. This can stem from their religious beliefs or their own convictions. For example, Christian fundamentalists, Muslim fundamentalists, as well as fundamentalists of other various religions, reject relativism, sexual promiscuity, pluralism and an unconditional tolerance. As a result, fundamentals as a whole are continuously accused of intolerance. This is without doubt the key phrase used by those pursuing these liberal, promiscuous freedoms. One often senses that those who make these accusations are the most intolerant. If all things be allowed, why not hold fast to those values that have been proven beneficial? Those who would forbid these values are just as intolerant dogmatic, as they refuse to allow others to have their own convictions. As a result, liberalism contradicts its own principles.

The term "fundamentalism" stems from a protestant movement in the USA at the beginning of the twentieth century. Back then, there was a resistance to the liberal tendencies that were creeping into the churches. Something that in my opinion, was right. Leading conservative theologians from the US and other countries issued a series of writings titled, "The Fundamentals". These writings laid down five foundational truths of the Christian faith that were to be upheld. These were:

1. The bible's infallibility
2. The deity of Jesus Christ
3. Jesus' virgin birth by Mary
4. The atoning work of Jesus Christ on the cross
5. The bodily resurrection of the dead at Christ's return

I ask you: Are these sectarian doctrines? No. These are clearly foundational, biblical teachings that many Christians and many churches have held fast to over the years. So to attach a picture of a narrow-minded dictator to the term fundamentalist is unjustified. Those opposing biblical Christianity and followers of other religions extend the term "fundamentalist" to other movements as well. In Islam, for example, the Muslim brotherhood is called fundamentalist. Their aim is to erect an Islamic State that resists the secular system of law, to make Islamic law binding. We see similar efforts among the so-called Hindu fundamentalists to restore a Great India, and make all men Hindus.

There is also Jewish fundamentalism which has two opposing viewpoints. The Zionists see in the modern state of Israel, the revival of the biblical Israel. The Chassidim (the "pious" ones) reject the State of Israel. They are of the opinion that the existence of the state of Israel is not necessary for the coming of the Messiah. Even worse they believe that the existence of the State of Israel even prevents the coming of the Messiah. There are even Jews who consider themselves orthodox, who live in Israel and enjoy its security while at the same time, uniting with the Palestinians against Israel.

Christian Fundamentalists are not Terrorists

Continuing on with our subject let us deal with another decisive question. What is the difference between a Christian and a Muslim Fundamentalist? There is one very important difference as to pertaining to our discussion. That is, Christians are expected to conduct themselves in accordance with Christ's commandment to "love your enemies, bless those that curse you, and do good to those who hate you!" (Matthew 5:44) These commandments Christ gave in His sermon on the Mount to His disciples. No where in the New Testament are we taught to kill our enemies. A Muslim can not say that about the Koran. We even have a booklet with all of the passages of the Koran where one can find the command to kill. For this reason it is in no way accurate, nor is it fair to make a correlation between Christian and Muslim fundamentalists. Doing so compares peaceable bible-believing Christians to violent Muslims.

By making the word fundamentalism disreputable it becomes a club to crush biblical Christianity. To make matters worse, some Christians resist being labeled 'fundamentalists' due to this negative twist to its original, good meaning. Many resist this label because they themselves do not hold on to the infallibility of the Holy Scriptures. I feel that we should not discard this term. We should attempt to openly defend its original meaning and its roots, thereby distinguishing it from its false definitions. Many are called fundamentalists, who believe in the absolute infallibility of the bible, not only in matters of the faith and there lifestyles, but also in the areas of creationism, history, geography and science. (for example creation, and the flood). Regarding the creation I would like to note: Nothing is impossible for God! He could have made the world in a second so why is it impossible for Him to make it in six days?

How Christians are being tactically divided

Unfortunately we see this divisive work even amongst the biblical Christians. There is hardly any Christian group or organization that is exempt from it. To me this is a sad phenomenon of the last days. This divisive work of defaming biblical Christians will not be aimed at all Christians and fellowships simultaneously. Those who clearly realize the current political situation and speak out clearly will be targeted first. This will have its purposes. Firstly, it should not appear as if a type of "persecution" of Christians were taking place. At first only a few will be accused. (It is just like this in China. There is the accepted state church as a display to the world of its tolerance. What about the others who are secretly persecuted?) Secondly, this will cause mediocre "biblical" Christians to distance themselves from the "radicals". In this manner they can divide the camp of biblical Christians and isolate those who actively confess their faith. Already there are clear signs that they will have some success in these areas.

A code of conduct for conversions

I now want to address a difficult matter; a code of conduct for conversions. I can only call this a "preventative obedience". We saw this kind of obedience in Germany in light of a rising dictator. Many hastily subjected themselves to this dictatorship before it actually became a reality. It is not my intention to hurt anybody by this statement. It is even possible that many are not even aware of the far reaching consequences of these current events. For this reason I say: "Pay attention to the way that the Evangelical Alliance is headed!"

In the past, when head representatives of the World Alliance met with representatives of the Vatican and the Ecumenical World Council of Churches, there would have been protests. All of a sudden, everyone is working together on higher goals, whatever these may be. One of them is called "A code of conduct for conversions". Does this mean that we will have dictated to us what we are allowed and not allowed to say on the mission field? Undeniably there have been grievances. There were circumstances where people were forced to convert to Christendom and receive baptism. Yet, today, millions are being forced to become Muslim with the result that Christian voices raise in protest of the many lives that are lost at the hand of Islam.

However, there is a real danger of throwing out the "baby with the bath water" with the result that mission work will become utterly impossible. The aim is to eliminate any methods that could have "aggressive, offensive" elements. I will mention some examples.

First here are two quotes right from the source. On May 12-16, 2006 there was a meeting between the Vatican and the World Council of Churches in Geneva in Lariano / Italy. All representatives of the World Alliance were present. In closing, it was said, "Everyone has the right to invite someone to understand their faith. Yet, we affirm that no one should injure the religious feelings of another". (So far, so good; but then it was said:) "At the same time we emphasize that everyone who has the need to convert others to seek deliverance from this obsession."[22] This is a key phrase in order to understand what is really at stake. The need to convert others is considered an obsession. Indeed it is the Lord who coverts the hearts, but it is our duty to testify of Him. Here is a quote from the co-chairman of the ÖRK

---

[22] Cf. R. Moeller, On our way to a code of conduct for conversions? In: ZEITJOURNAL 4/2007, p. 35.

commission for faith and the church, Reverend Dr. Hermen Shastri: "The religious preachers must be told that no religion has a monopoly on the truth and there are many ways to salvation."[23]

In a paper stating there position, the Evangelical Fellowship of India (Evangelical Alliance of India) contained a list of offensive terms the use of which would no longer be allowed. There it says: "However, warfare words, such as army, advance, attack, battle, campaign, crusade, conquer, commandos, enemy, foe, forces, marching orders, mobilize, soldier, tactical plan, target, victory, weapons, have been wrongly used as motivational tools for missions. Other offensive words include pagan, darkness, and heathen. Emphasis on such vocabulary is unloving, inappropriate and counter-productive. Language that excludes women also offends. We must continuously examine both our attitudes and our language."[24] Are we no longer allowed to refer to the unconverted as heathen? That fits together with the quote earlier, that no one should have the "obsession to convert others".

Not only are those who are obedient God to be ostracized, but also all those who yet conduct missions and evangelizing in a clear and uncompromising fashion. Naturally there are black sheep that attempt to "buy" conversions by means of bribes. But hopefully we all agree that we are against such actions. Yet, can we just simply erase expressions like those on the coat of armor as mentioned in Ephesians 6? Our walk with the Lord is a battle with the enemy, the devil and all those who serve him. Are we not allowed to say that? We see that the antichristian developments are becoming more and more evident.

The Bible has prophesied all of these things

In order to have a biblical orientation on this theme, let us look at Paul's second letter to Timothy, chapter three. Here is becomes apparent that the bible is God's Word, as no man can know ahead of time what will transpire in the last days. We read:

"But realize this, that in the last days difficult times will come. For men will be lovers of self, lovers of money, boastful arrogant, revilers, disobedient to parents, ungrateful, unholy, unloving irreconcilable, malicious gossips, without self-control, brutal, haters of good, treacherous, reckless, conceited, lovers of pleasure rather than lovers of God; holding to a form of godliness, although they have denied its power; and avoid such men as these."

Verse 12 goes on to say: "And indeed, all who desire to live godly in Christ Jesus will suffer persecution. But evil men and impostors will proceed from bad to worse, deceiving and being deceived. You, however, continue in the things you have learned and become convinced of, knowing from whom you have learned them; and that from childhood you have known the sacred writings which are able to give you the wisdom that leads to salvation through faith which is in Christ Jesus. All Scripture is inspired by God and profitable for teaching, for reproof, for correction, for training in righteousness; that the man of God may be adequate, equipped for every good work."

Here it very clearly tells of the last days. They will be days of obsession. The Greek words – kairoi chalepoi - mean obsessed days. In these end times, people will indulge themselves in the occult, fornication and sin. We experience this in all kinds of blasphemous novels and films. In particular I want to pick out the 2006 novel and movie "The Sacrilege" ("The Da Vinci Code"). In these the Jesus Christ as the Son of God was refuted. Jesus was supposedly just a man who even fathered children

---

[23] Cf. . Moeller, On our way to a code of conduct for conversions? In the ZEITJOURNAL Magazine 4/2007, p. 36.
[24] Ibid p.39

whose offspring are still around. On 06.06.2006 a make over of the movie "The Omen" was opened in cinemas. This movie depicts the rise of the Antichrist and 666. Eerie things are really taking place. The condition of our societies unfortunately makes these types of things bestsellers. For children the bestseller is "Harry Potter" and for the adults it is the "Sacrilege". The meaning of the word sacrilege is desecration. The book of Revelation (21:8) tells us clearly that no one who loves to commit sin will have a place in God's kingdom. Let this be a warning in view of these types of books and movies.

Satan's double Strategy

The enemy of our soul needs a two-fold strategy to fight the church of Jesus Christ. His first weapon is outward pressure to include a bloody persecution like that which raged through the early church by the hand of the Roman Empire. Even now, where the antichristian era draws to a close, one may observe Christian persecution. One has just to think about the former Soviet Union, North Korea, China and many Muslim countries.

When bloody persecution does not avail, then the enemy's second tactic is seduction. The devil seduces Christians away from the life giving faith and from the narrow path which leads us through the narrow gate (Matthew 7:14). Thereby they are drawn onto the broad path. This is done by preaching them a modern, worldly Christianity that shimmers and glitters with the various forms of "worship" using rock music, movies, shows, dance and theater. This can be seen in Willow Creek, Saddleback, Emerging Church and others. Those who submit themselves to this seduction do not even realize how true the following statement becomes: "When we bring the world into the church, the church becomes the world".

Many Christians are not willing to take this matter seriously. As a result, many churches are very worldly. One attempts with these methods to reach out to people by "meeting them on their terms", as is so often said. This however is the wrong way. These worldly methods water down the gospel. We must clearly preach a holy and merciful God as the core of the gospel, as our church fathers and the reformers did, without the worldly trash. Otherwise we give the impression that Christianity is a program for entertainment with the redemptive work of the cross as some blasphemous climax. This is a very evil, wicked twisting of the Gospel of Christ. So the tactics of the adversary to destroy Jesus' church are persecution and seduction. God allows these to sift out His church, for we know that the true church of Jesus Christ can not be destroyed: ... and the gates of hell shall not prevail against her - Jesus' bridal church. (Matthew 16:18b)

Persecution unites, seduction divides the church

Persecution unites and bonds the church together. The true, born again believers out of the various denominations will hold together when persecution comes; where as seduction divides the church. We experience this almost everywhere regardless of denomination or confession. Everywhere churches are splitting up. I am often invited to remnant churches or house groups that have left their church, due to the inability to endure the worldly spirit penetrating that church. This seduction begins with a mild criticism of certain bible teachings as taught in more and more "conservative" seminaries and bible schools. The criticism has the opinion that some of the questionable teachings coming from the Universities should be adopted in order to be more modern and knowledgeable. As a result we see a diminishing in number of true biblically sound bible schools.

Seduction divides the church. Persecution unites her. Seduction allows the counterfeit to triumph. Persecution purges out the fake, leaving only the faithful ones to stay together. It is not without reason that Jesus Christ said that the pathway to the kingdom of God is narrow, and the gate is narrow. The way to the kingdom of God is not a broad path. It is indeed not "Broadway". Many live in an illusion that they are Christians when they really are not. They are not walking the narrow path. That is the message of "holiness" is so decisive. Holiness is the mark of true Christianity. There is a reason that God's Word admonishes us to remove the leaven of sin from our lives, - and our churches. This cleansing must begin in our own hearts; in mine and yours. Remember, a little leaven leavens the whole lump! (I Corinthians 5)

Will the approaching persecution of Christians in Europe reveal who is a genuine Christian versus those who are Christians by name only? One can only hope so. May the Lord God grant each individual Christian the strength to remain a Christian even if it may cost them something? This price may be our honor, our freedom or maybe even our lives, as it is have been under communism and Islam.

Stand Fast!

Now, here are a few words from our Lord Jesus Christ for our comfort and strengthening. In Luke 21: 18-19 the Lord says: "Yet not a hair of your head will perish. By your endurance you will gain your lives." What a comfort! Jesus also tells us that he will give us irresistible, irrefutable wisdom before our enemies when we face trials and persecution. (Luke 21:15) We are not even supposed to contemplate what we are going to say. Much rather we must trust that the Lord by His Holy Spirit will give us the right words to say when we are called to give an account. Even if we should be sentenced to death, the words in Matthew 10; 28 apply: "And do not fear those who kill the body, but are unable to kill the soul: but rather fear Him who is able to destroy both soul and body in hell." And 39: "He who has found his life shall lose it, and he who has lost his life for My sake shall find it."

I know it is easy to quote these passages. Yet, I am convinced that when we are in the midst of persecution, whether in Europe or wherever in the world, the Lord will give His strength.

Obey God rather than Man

How should we conduct ourselves? What can we do in light of these current developments? Again I repeat the words of our Lord that not a hair on our head will perish without God's permission. The Lord will give us wisdom as to what we should say. We must hold fast to these promises. We will get lonelier and lonelier, even amongst Christians. This sad development is probably the heaviest of burdens.

In this light, passage from Acts 5:29 gains in significance: "We must obey God rather than men." Indeed we want to obey and faithfully submit to the governing authorities. However, in Acts 5:27-33 we are taught the limits to this obedience: "And when they had brought them (the apostles), before the Council. And the high priest questioned them, saying, "We gave you strict orders not to continue teaching in this name (the name of Jesus), and behold, you have filled Jerusalem with your teaching, and intend to bring this man's blood (the blood of Jesus) upon us." But Peter and the apostles answered and said: "We must obey God rather than men … the God of our fathers raised up Jesus, whom you had put to death by hanging Him on a cross. He is the one whom God exalted to His right hand as a Prince and a Savior, to grant repentance to Israel and forgiveness of sins. And we are witnesses of theses things; and so is the Holy Spirit, whom God has given to those who obey Him." But when they heard this, they were cut to the quick and were intending to slay them."

Here were orders that contradicted the commission that God gave to His people. The high priests attempted to silence the disciples. They were told to no longer talk or preach about Jesus. It is interesting who wanted this prohibited. It was the leaders of the religious sector; the Council! Today they would be called the church leaders. When Peter preached at Pentecost (Acts 2), the people were "cut to the heart" but in a good way, as it lead them to salvation! They repented and were baptized. In the bible passage above, the apostles' answer so angered the Sanhedrin that they thought to kill them. It is awesome, how blind the religious leaders were. First they crucified Jesus Christ. Then they proceeded to persecute the disciples who proclaimed him as the resurrected Savior of the world. Jesus did not remain in the grave. He has truly risen! We, too, want to testify to of this.

Thomas Zimmermanns writes in his book "Christians under pressure": "The Christian church is obligated to preach the Word to it's members, and 'not just the pure Word but the whole Word of God.'(Richard Wurmbrand) She was unfaithful to her duty when she removed certain biblical truths from her message."

It has become very unpopular to speak about judgment, damnation, hell and repentance. However, we may not eliminate these truths when we speak of the love of God. The love of God shines there the brightest when we have come to recognize, and acknowledge, the lost state that Jesus saved us from by His blood.

Zimmermanns continues:

"There is nothing spiritual or matter of fact about the desire to avoid defamation and the loss of prestige in public. These are purely carnal motives. This not only applies to our message to the church. It also concerns the stand we take towards the government and society regarding the law and the gospel".

I will close this section with a further sentence from Zimmermanns:

"Even if the State should make all kinds of laws and rules; the church still may not deviate from her true mission, otherwise she is being lead into sin and disobedience. Here again the word from Acts 5:29 applies: We must obey God rather than men!"

From Defensive to Offensive

We can not just put our heads in the sand, much rather we must resist as long as possible. If this means, they put us in prison, we need to be ready for that also. We are challenged to be an influence as long as there is time in schools, in the media etc. The various Christians should work together. Of course I emphasize, this can not be at the expense of biblical truth. I do not recommend a big coalition of all confessions as some would propagate. Rather I encourage the coming together of all those who are truly born again by the spirit of God despite any differences in individual teachings with this goal in mind.

Continuous accusations are made that we are narrow minded, intolerant, old fashioned and legalistic, while others, present themselves as advanced, modern, and tolerant and pluralistic. This is not true! We clearly proclaim the very best message about the very best way for people to be saved and to get there lives right with God. It is by our redeemer, the Lord Jesus Christ that their lives receive a new perspective.
May the Lord Jesus give us strength, when again it will cost us something to be a Christian.

A Personal Word

In case you have never really read the bible, then I heartily invite you to do so. Seek Jesus Christ in the Word of God and in prayer. Come to him with all of your burdens and with all of your sins. HE loves you. He wants to grant you forgiveness for your sins and lead you to everlasting life. Read in the bible about who Jesus is, and what he did for you. Read how he gave HIS life as a sacrifice for the guilt of the world. Jesus died on the cross in order to wash you clean from all the guilt and evil in your life. This is the mystery of the faith: Jesus died in order to reconcile us to God. HE rose from the dead and lives and wants to live in our lives by HIS presence. Let HIM reign in your life and HE will lead your way gloriously. The choice is eternal life with Jesus or eternal torment in hell. Only Jesus Christ can save you and give you a life that pleases God. It is God's will that you be saved. Do you not want this, too?
This has nothing to do with theological discussions, but everything to do with the fundamentals of our existence. The disciples were willing to give up all they had for Jesus' sake and to offer up their lives.
One must obey God more than people!

Let us pray!

Dear heavenly Father, we come to you in the name of your beloved Son Jesus Christ and worship you. Thank you that you sent us your son to redeem us from sin, death and the devil. Thank you that we may have your word which reveals to us the whole truth, and everything that we need for our life and for our death. Keep us in your hand, especially as the shadows of these last days grow longer and your church must suffer hardship and distress. Help us when it will cost us something to proclaim your Word with all clarity. Protect all who still want to preach Your unadulterated Word. Let us not take anything away from Your Truth. Much rather let us confess and proclaim you as redeemer and Lord. Please give us yet a time of grace, and hold back your judgments. Grant that those who are governing us, will change their thoughts and plans. You can work miracles. Please save many still in this time of grace, that they will become your children and receive eternal life. We want to give you all honor, Holy, Almighty and merciful Father in Heaven. In Jesus Name, Amen

Appendix:

The Treaty of Lisbon – the End of Liberty in Europe?

With this essay I want to prove the following hypothesis:

The European Union is in great danger of developing into a dictatorship.

Reasons:

1. Only very few countries asked their population if they wanted to join the EU.

2. All significant, important decisions have been centralized to the EU.

3. The population of the individual countries and their national parliaments has hardly any possibility of influencing the European legislation.

4. The EU has already given itself totalitarian authority in all important facets, whether they are political, economical or judicial in nature.

5. The member countries give up more and more of their sovereignty to the EU.

6. The Laws of the individual countries have to make room to the European Law.

7. The High Courts of each country must forfeit their competencies to the European Tribunal.

8. The EU seeks to build up and arm a European Army.

9. Consequences of EU policy can be restrictions on our freedom of speech and our freedom to have an opinion.

10. The Preamble and the basic values of the as defined in the Treaty of the European Union stand in opposition to the Christian faith in many important points. Especially the Clauses pertaining to discrimination can ignite a persecution of Christians.

For Europe, but against the EU

Continental Europe and the European Union are not one and the same thing. The present EU is a conglomeration of various European countries which have come together for the purpose of establishing a unified government for Europe as a whole.

As Christians we desire peace and a harmonious cooperation amongst the European people and their countries. We must, however, turn away from a European Union as it is currently developing with its centralization, its anti democratic tendencies, and its restrictions on our freedom of speech and our freedom to preach as Christians. Furthermore, we must reject a Europe without God, as it is anchored in the Treaty. A super-state, a mammoth-sized institution is forming that offers no real freedoms to its individual states or its individual citizens. Already most of our laws are made in Brussels and not in Berlin, or any other European capitol. National law is on the retreat, handing more and more authority over to European Law. I will yet confirm this.

A desirable alternative would be, to have an alliance of countries with equal rights being given to the individual States and the individual citizens. This union should be limited to essentials, necessary for a peaceable cooperation which furthers a good neighborly coexistence. It would be better to strive for a decentralized network of independent, friendly states, rather than centralization.

The Incapacitation of the citizens

Only few countries were even allowed to vote about joining the EU or to vote on its Treaty.

Of all 27 countries now members of the EU, only Ireland, voted on the Treaty. On June 13, 2008, the citizens of Ireland voted down the Treaty. This was a result of aroused citizens who went door to door informing others of the contents the Treaty of Lisbon, a treaty which had been negotiated behind closed doors. The Irish voted down the treaty although they were nearly "blackmailed" into accepting it. "The text of the Treaty was not released until April 16, 2008, to prevent any juicy details from getting too much publicity... The Irish were reminded of the fact that in the past, the EU given billions in aid....accepting the Treaty would be rewarded, but rejecting it would be penalized by cutting off the aid." (A press report from the German Central Party in June 2008)

 Despite this outcome the Treaty is to be put into affect. In 2005 both France and the Netherlands had rejected the Treaty. After this defeat, another Treaty was constructed having very few differences to the old one. This new treaty, though, would no longer need to be voted on by citizens of the member countries. Only the Irish voted, and they rejected it.

The attorney, Professor Schachtschneider, wrote this on this event: "The referendum in Ireland was an act of freedom that defended this right to be part of the decision making process for all citizens of the EU. Now the outrage of the politicians toward the Irish, who dared to say "no" to the Treaty of Lisbon displays their lack of regard for the general public. Even the manner, in which the Treaty was agreed upon, after it was turned down in France and the Netherlands, is in view of democracy, a scandal. As long as the possibility for everyone to vote on the Union' progression toward becoming a Superpower, we do not live in a democratic republic that strives for freedom and justice. Instead, we live in a State, ruled by authoritative parties. The Irish will be forced to vote again. Alone for this reason, the oppression coming from the Eurocrats must be openly opposed by various means of publicity, like elections and hearings etc." (Zeit-Fragen Online, 2.8.2008)

The Treaty of the European Union without God

We will take a look at the consolidated version of the Treaty.

The Preamble: "DRAWING INSPIRATION from the cultural, religious and humanist inheritance of Europe, from which have developed the universal values ..." There is absolutely no reference to God. The God of the bible can never be understood as a religion. The Christian faith is the revelation of the living God and not a man-made religion. As a result the Christian faith can not be found in the Treaty.

Unchristian Values

Article 2: "The Union is founded on the values of respect for human dignity, freedom, democracy, equality, the rule of law and respect for human rights, including the rights of persons belonging to minorities. These values are common to the Member States in a society in which pluralism, non-discrimination, tolerance, justice, solidarity and equality between women and men prevail."

Here we find a philosophical enlightenment containing no absolute truth and no godly revelation. Any absolute truths are replaced by pluralism and other definitions of tolerance as found in the handwritings of freemasonry. Even the natural differences of the genders, as originally intended by God are to put aside. The equality that is meant here is the antichristian ideology of Gender Mainstreaming with the marriage of homosexual couples as a consequence. In contrast to accepting biological gender as intended by God, gender mainstreaming promotes gender self-determination. Gender mainstreaming is a self-exalting attempt to take the matter of determining one's gender (or sex) into one's own hands, to include the style of dress and sex-change operations, an initiation of feminist and Marxist movements. Consequently, gender mainstreaming is firmly anchored in the homosexual and lesbian movements. Gender mainstreaming is, biblically speaking, sin and doomed to failure. Yet, this is to be a fundamental value in the European Union by which everything else is evaluated!

The Battle against Discrimination

Art 3, § 2: "The Union shall combat social exclusion and discrimination, and shall promote social justice and protection, equality between women and men, solidarity between generations and protection of the rights of the child." Unfortunately the rights of the unborn are not protected! Without doubt, we should refuse to discriminate against someone by way of snubbing or slurring them. When we, as Christians call such practices, like homosexuality, sin, we are only quoting the Word of God. (See Rom. 1, I Cor. 6 etc) This is done to help people by pointing them to Jesus Christ and His love, which alone can heal and forgive them by granting repentance. The Lord Jesus can heal people who live in sin and renew their lives. Is this to be battled and forbidden?

The New World Order

Art. 21, (The goal of the European Union) in § H: The goal is to "promote an international system based on stronger multilateral cooperation and good global governance."

We see here that Europe is just a preliminary step to a global "One World". The main author of this Treaty is Valery Giscard d'Estaing, a free mason of high degree. His handwriting is clearly seen in this Treaty. There may be no mention of God, only of Religion. Everything must remain relative.

Military Armament

It may surprise some to know that parallel to the EU's striving for a "pseudo"-tolerance, it is also seeking to build up its own army. Art. 42, §3: "Member States shall make civilian and military capabilities available to the Union for the implementation of the common security and defense policy, to contribute to the objectives defined by the Council. Those Member States which together establish multinational forces may also make them available to the common security and defense policy. Member States shall undertake progressively to improve their military capabilities. The Agency in the field of defense capabilities development, research, acquisition and armaments (hereinafter referred to as 'the European Defense Agency') shall identify operational requirements, shall promote measures to satisfy those requirements, shall contribute to identifying and, where appropriate, implementing any measure needed to strengthen the industrial and technological base of the defense sector, shall participate in defining a European capabilities and armaments policy, and shall assist the Council in evaluating the improvement of military capabilities."

Art 43, §1: " The tasks referred to in Article 42(1), in the course of which the Union may use civilian and military means, shall include joint disarmament operations, humanitarian and rescue tasks, military advice and assistance tasks, conflict prevention and peace-keeping tasks, tasks of combat forces in crisis management, including peace-making and post-conflict stabilization. All these tasks may contribute to the fight against terrorism, including by supporting third countries in combating terrorism in their territories. "

Where as in Article 42 they talk about the progressive improvement of the military capabilities, in Article 43 they talk of joint disarmament operations. These apparent contradictions camouflage the same time the true nature of this matter. Under the motto of "the fight against terrorism", Europe will commit itself to the war on terrorism (whatever that truly means) and will use this fact to build up arms. The foreign minister of the European Union receives a tremendous amount of power and influence. The Treaty of the EU awards this minister with an extraordinary declaration as read in Art. 43 §2: " The High Representative of the Union for Foreign Affairs and Security Policy, acting under the authority of the Council and in close and constant contact with the Political and Security Committee, shall ensure coordination of the civilian and military aspects of such tasks."

The Law empowers the EU with Authority

The European Union is to take on the form of a nation with an internal market and its own foreign minister. In Art.45 we read: The Union shall have "legal personality". Hereby the direct connection becomes visible, what Professor Schachtschneider brings up in his case against what he calls the "Law empowering the EU with authority".

Article 48, §2: "The Government of any Member State, the European Parliament or the Commission may submit to the Council proposals for the amendment of the Treaties. These proposals may, inter alia, serve either to increase or to reduce the competences conferred on the Union in the Treaties. These proposals shall be submitted to the European Council by the Council and the national Parliaments shall be notified." One reads exactly this that the national parliaments shall merely "be notified" of the plans and the decisions being made by their governments together with top level EU officials. Similar wording is found in the so-called "flexibility clause", Article 352 of the Treaty on the Functioning of the EU, which will be covered shortly.

The Treaty of Lisbon is divided into two, equally binding parts. There is the Treaty of the European Union (TEU) and the Treaty on the Functioning of the European Union (TFEU). The TEU addresses many of the formal matters, like the various governing bodies. We will concentrate now on the TFEU which differentiates the competences. There is the exclusive competence and the shared competence.

Art. 2, § 1 (Categories and areas of Union competence) "...the Treaties confer on the Union exclusive competence in a specific area, only the Union may legislate and adopt legally binding acts, the Member States being able to do so themselves only if so empowered by the Union or for the implementation of Union acts."

Art. 2, § 2: "...the Treaties confer on the Union a competence shared with the Member States in a specific area, the Union and the Member States may legislate and adopt legally binding acts in that area. The Member States shall exercise their competence to the extent that the Union has not exercised its competence." The fact, to the extent that a competence is conferred, that which has been conferred on the Union has precedence, even in shared competencies! This is very important to keep in mind!

Art. 3, § 1 a-e: "The Union shall have exclusive competence in the following areas: customs union; the establishing of the competition rules necessary for the functioning of the internal market; monetary policy for the Member States whose currency is the Euro; the conservation of marine biological resources under the common fisheries policy; common commercial policy."

Paragraph 2: "The Union shall also have exclusive competence for the conclusion of an international agreement when its conclusion is provided for in a legislative act of the Union or is necessary to enable the Union to exercise its internal competence, or insofar as its conclusion may affect common rules or alter their scope."

Shared competences deal with all other areas. Art. 4 names: the internal market; social policy, for the aspects defined in this Treaty; economic, social, and territorial cohesion; agriculture and fisheries, excluding the conservation of marine biological resources; environment; consumer protection; transportation; trans-European networks; energy; area of freedom security and justice; common safety concerns in public health matters, for the aspects defined in this Treaty.

This puts the law of justice into Europe's hand. This is decisively affirmed by the Declarations Annexed to the Final Act of the Treaty, the Declaration on Article 16 (9),point 17 (the Declaration Concerning Primacy: "The Opinion of the Council Legal Service of 22 June 2007, it results from the case-law of the Court of Justice that primacy of EC law is a cornerstone principle of Community law. According to the Court, this principle is inherent to the specific nature of the European Community. At the time of the first judgment of this established case law there was no mention of primacy in the treaty.

It is still the case today. The fact that the principle of primacy will not be included in the future treaty shall not in any way change the existence of the principle and the existing case-law of the Court of Justice. "

A Double Standard

As set down in the TFEU (Treaty on the Functioning of the EU), the ideology of gender mainstreaming will find wide support with a massive fight against discrimination against this. Simultaneously churches and other religious associations will be merely regarded, while obvious attempts are being made to convince them of the correctness of EU policies.

Art. 8: "In all its activities, the Union shall aim to eliminate inequalities, and to promote equality, between men and women." (Gender mainstreaming)

Art. 10: "In defining and implementing its policies and activities, the Union shall aim to combat discrimination based on sex racial or ethnic origin, religion or belief, disability, age or sexual orientation."

Art. 17: "The Union respects and does not prejudice the status under national law of churches and religious associations or communities in the Member States. The Union equally respects the status under national law of philosophical and non-confessional organizations. Recognizing their identity and their specific contribution, the Union shall maintain an open, transparent and regular dialogue with these churches and organizations."

The European Arrest Warrant

The following can also be read in the TFEU:

Art. 67, § 3: "The Union shall endeavor to ensure a high level of security through measures to prevent and combat crime, racism and xenophobia, and through measures for coordination and cooperation between police and judicial authorities and other competent authorities, as well as through the mutual recognition of judgments in criminal matters and, if necessary, through the approximation of criminal laws."

Art. 75: Where necessary to achieve the objectives set out in Article 67, as regard preventing and combating terrorism and related activities, the European Parliament and the Council, acting in accordance with the ordinary legislative procedure, shall define a framework for administrative measures with regard to capital movements and payments such as the freezing of funds, financial assets or economic gains belonging to, or owned or held by, natural or legal persons, groups or non-State entities."

Charges, Sanctions and fines

The Treaty on the Functioning of the EU also includes severe sanctions against those member-states which are Either insolvent or do not fit into the system:

Article 126, § 11: "As long as a Member State fails to comply with a decision taken in accordance with paragraph 9, the Council may decide to apply or, as the case may be, intensify one or more of the following measures ... to impose fines of an appropriate size."

Punishment is imposed by the Council in Brussels, if a certain state has a financial deficit which does not correspond to its general balance toward Europe.

Article 136, § 3: "Within the limits and under the conditions adopted by the Council under the procedure laid down in Article 129, the European Central Bank shall be entitled to impose fines or periodic penalty payments on undertakings for failure to comply with obligations under its regulations and decisions."

The European Union and the United Nations

Only the UN (United Nations) has a higher position than that of the EU and represents the supreme institution for creating a "One World". The EU and the UN also cooperate militarily. The exact schedule for this building up of arms is conspicuous.

Article 220: "The Union shall establish all appropriate forms of cooperation with the organs of the United Nations ... The High Representative of the Union for Foreign Affairs and Security Policy and the Commission shall be instructed to implement this Article."

Protocol 10, 1b: "... have the capacity to supply by 2010 at the latest, either at national level or as a component of multinational force groups, targeted combat units from the missions planned, structured at a tactical level as a battle group, with support elements including transport and logistics, capable of carrying out the tasks referred to in Article 43 of the Treaty on European Union, within a period of 5 to 30 days, in particular in response to requests from the United Nations Organization, and which can be sustained for an initial period of 30 days and be extended up to at least 120 days."

By the way, all the UN-resolutions concerning the Middle East so far have been directed against Israel. This reminds us of Zechariah, chapter 12 and 14, where it says that in the last days all peoples on earth will march against Israel.

The Petition of Professor Schachtschneider against the EU-Treaties

On May 27, 2005 the german Prof. Karl Albrecht Schachtschneider addressed his petition[25] against the EU-Treaty to the Federal Constitutional Court of Germany. Prof. Schachtschneider complains that the law requiring approval (that which is to approve the Treaty) is unconstitutional as it violates the democratic, social and national principles as established by the structural principles of the Federal Republic of Germany (like other countries, too). This treaty legitimizes the replacement of the German

---

[25] Karl Albrecht Schachtschneider, Organklage, Verfassungsbeschwerde, Antrag auf andere Abhilfe, Antrag auf einstweilige Anordnung des Mitglieds des Deutschen Bundestages, Bayer. Staatsminister a.D. Dr. Peter Gauweiler ... gegen den Deutschen Bundestag, vertreten durch den Präsidenten des Deutschen Bundestages, Wolfgang Thierse ... und die Bundesrepublik Deutschland, vertreten durch die Bundesregierung, diese vertreten durch den Bundeskanzler ..., 27th may, 2005.

Basic Law with the European Law. This kind of far reaching decision can not just be voted on by a governing body that was elected by the people but the people themselves must vote on this. And this, a referendum, is to be denied most European people. A referendum would be a politically, important demand to be made, as it was allowed in Ireland.

Professor Schachtschneider also complains that this approving law is also contrary to the German nation (and other nations). German nationality is to be constricted as far as possible to favor an existential European nationality. The national parliaments are no longer accountable for policies made. Thus, the political decision-making process is removing itself more and more from the democratic principles, which are necessary to maintain a balance in power. In this manner it is becoming totalitarian. That, which was originally intended to be a community for commerce, now wants to control every aspect of the countries. But we can not just be delivered over to a bureaucratic system that is only run by the heads of States and no longer relies upon a basic decision making foundation.

Professor Schachtschneider demands more democracy through Referendums and the likes, versus less democracy. He also insists that Germany or other countries should not agree to any treaty or contract that oversteps relinquishes their own areas of competencies, especially if these agreements contribute to the removal, or limitation of national sovereignty.

Schachtschneider also points out in a warning fashion, the continuous increase in power of the European Courts, as well as its influence in the policies of foreign affairs, security, and defense to include the establishing of European armed forces.

Expert opinion of Professor Murswiek on the Treaty of Lisbon

(Prof. Dr. Dietrich Murswiek is professor for constitutional, administrative and international law at the University of Freiburg, southern Germany.)

In his expert opinion[26], as was submitted at the German Constitutional Court in 2008, Prof. Dietrich Murswiek referred to a former sentence of the same court dating back to 1992/1993, in which a list of minimal requirements was set up to be met by the European Union. But as a matter of fact, most of these criteria (as stated below) do no longer apply:

1. The European Union may not constitute a state in itself, but only a federation of states. - Now it shall become a state.

2. The EU should be restricted to an economic union. - Now it becomes a political and legal union and, let me add, even an ideological union.

3. The member states shall remain sovereign over their treaties. - Now they are deprived of their power.

4. The EU should be granted only limited competence according to the principle of limited authorization in each individual case. - Through the constitutional treaty the EU now grants to itself a total authorization.

5. The EU should respect the sovereignty of its states in that they should have the right to withdraw from the union. - It is true that this right is included in the Treaty of Lisbon but states who want to make use of this option

---

[26] Dietrich Murswiek, Gutachten zum Vertrag von Lissabon, Mai 2008.

will, in practice, face negative consequences.

6. The EU should not be granted the authority to neither institute on its own new areas of competence for itself nor rob national states of their competence. - But this is exactly what happens by means of the law of authorization (see above) and the clause of flexibility (see below).

Prof. Murswiek concludes: "Up to this day the EU has occupied central areas of national sovereignty. It aspires to a state-like character for itself."

The new legislation makes it possible for the Union to enlarge its competences by means of the so-called Flexibility Clause.

Article 352: "If action by the Union should prove necessary, within the framework of the policies defined by the Treaties, to attain one of the objectives set out in the Treaties, and the Treaties have not provided the necessary powers, the Council, acting unanimously on a proposal from the Commission and after obtaining the consent of the European Parliament, shall adopt the appropriate measures. Where the measures in question are adopted by the Council in accordance with a special legislative procedure, it shall also act unanimously on a proposal from the Commission and after obtaining the consent of the European Parliament."

Prof. Murswiek points out: "As legal competences are shifted to Brussels, the national governments gain an overwhelming power in relation to their respective parliaments." Potential new laws which do not find a majority on the national level can be put into force via the European institutions thus circumventing the national parliament. A minister, who does not obtain the consent of his parliament for a desired new law, may propose a new EU-regulation to the same effect in the EU-commission. If he manages to come to an agreement with his colleagues within the conference of ministers, they will make a resolution for this new regulation which then will easily pass the European administration. Eventually the national public including its parliament will become aware of that new law – only in the moment when it is already in effect.

Will Europe thus become a dictatorship?

The former president of the German Constitutional Court and former German Federal President, Roman Herzog, is today one of the sharpest critics of the EU-constitution although he himself had a major role in drawing up the EU-Charta. Early in 2007 he explained why, when he wrote in a newspaper article (WELT am Sonntag, 14.1.2007) under the headline *"The European Union jeopardizes parliamentary democracy in Germany"*:

"An impenetrable, complex and entangled giant institution has formed, which reaches out for more and more areas of competence and control." - Here we can clearly see the danger of an emerging dictatorship for every country in Europe.

May GOD protect the European nations!
And may many people resist the emerging dictatorship!

9 781798 183403